W9-AJO-212

HUMMINGBIRDS

LIVING WILD

LIVING WILD

Published by Creative Education
P.O. Box 227, Mankato, Minnesota 56002
Creative Education is an imprint of The Creative Company
www.thecreativecompany.us

Design and production by Mary Herrmann
Art direction by Rita Marshall
Printed by Corporate Graphics in the United States of America

Photographs by 123RF (Marie Daloia, Luis Cesar Tejo), Alamy (Derrick Alderman, Lee Dalton, Danita Delimont, Krystyna Szulecka Photography, David Lingard, Rolf Nussbaumer Photography), Corbis (Tim Davis, Werner Forman, Thomas Kitchin & Victoria Hurst/Wave, Gianni Dagli Orti), Dreamstime (Baburns, Steve Byland, Judy Kennamer, Ludek Lukac, Naturedisplay, Dewald Reiners, Rinusbaak), Getty Images (Felipe Davalos/National Geographic, DEA Picture Library, Frans Lemmens), iStockphoto (David L Amsler, Pattie Calfy, Missing35mm, Frank Pali, Shelly Perry, John Pitcher, Glenn Robertson, Paul Tessier, Jarno Gonzalez Zarraonandia)

Library of Congress Cataloging-in-Publication Data
Gish, Melissa.
Hummingbirds / by Melissa Gish.
p. cm. — (Living wild)
Includes bibliographical references and index.
Summary: A look at hummingbirds, including their habitats, physical characteristics such as their ability to hover, behaviors, relationships with humans, and admired status in the world today.
ISBN 978-1-60818-078-3
1. Hummingbirds—Juvenile literature. I. Title.

QL696.A558G57 2011
598.7'64—dc22   2010028314

CPSIA: 052112 PO1577

9 8 7 6 5 4 3

CREATIVE EDUCATION

HUMMINGBIRDS

Melissa Gish

It is late June, and the sun has risen on a dewy meadow. Above a sea of wildflowers, butterflies bob like tiny sailboats on invisible waves.

It is late June, and the sun has risen on a dewy meadow. Above a sea of wildflowers, butterflies bob like tiny sailboats on invisible waves. Bees dance in midair around tall stalks of showy goldenrod and slender stems of purple coneflowers, pausing to hug each brilliant bloom and gather powdery **pollen** on their legs. Like gems tossed into the air, two ruby-throated hummingbirds flash upward and then seem to fall, diving together toward the clustered blossoms of a blazing-orange butterfly weed. Two male hummingbirds will not share a feeding spot, though, and the birds begin to fight for territory. One flies straight at the other, who quickly flits upward. The rivals chase each other around the butterfly weed, zooming and diving at each other for several minutes until one of them gives up and zooms away to find a different patch of sugary sweet flower blossoms on which to feed.

WHERE IN THE WORLD THEY LIVE

■ Ruby-throated Hummingbird
eastern and midwestern North America

■ Marvelous Spatuletail Hummingbird
northern Peru

■ Coquette Hummingbird
Central America

■ Gorgeted Puffleg Hummingbird
Colombia

■ Sword-billed Hummingbird
northern South America

■ Broad-tailed Hummingbird
southern and western North America

■ Hermit Hummingbird
southern Mexico to Argentina

■ Purple-throated Carib Hummingbird
islands of the Lesser Antilles

The more than 320 species of hummingbird are spread throughout the western half of the world, from southern Alaska to Argentina. The South American country of Colombia houses the greatest number—160 different species—while its neighbor, Ecuador, is home to about 130. The colored squares represent some common general locations of eight hummingbird species living in the world today.

JEWELS OF THE SKY

Hummingbirds are the smallest birds on Earth, and their brilliantly colored **plumage** and unique flying techniques make them some of the most fascinating and beautiful creatures on the planet. Hummingbirds appear in virtually every color of the rainbow. Their feathers are iridescent, which means that light reflected off their surfaces creates shimmering variations in color, much like a soap bubble. Hummingbirds are named for the humming sound generated by their wings in flight. More than 320 species of hummingbird exist in the family Trochilidae, a name derived from the ancient Greek word *trochilos*, meaning "small bird." This bird family is second only to the flycatchers in its number of members.

Hummingbirds are found throughout the Western Hemisphere, from Alaska to Argentina, but most species live in South America, and fewer than 20 species live in North America. Many northern species migrate. Males begin their migration a few weeks before females so they can secure good territories with plentiful food for their mates. Each fall, the ruby-throated hummingbird migrates

The green violet-ear of Mexico and Central America can be found at elevations of up to 13,000 feet (3,962 m).

The Spanish first called hummingbirds *joyas voladores* (*HOY-as voh-lah-DOH-rehs*), or "flying jewels."

Most mammals have 7 cervical vertebrae, or neck bones, but hummingbirds may have 14 or 15.

The male tooth-billed hummingbird's beak has sharp spikes and a hook for pulling insects from leaves and tree cavities.

from eastern North America to its winter home in Central America, traveling an average of 20 miles (32 km) per day.

The closest relatives of hummingbirds are swifts. These two groups of birds belong to the order Apodiformes, a word that means "footless." Although they have small, weak feet, members of this order do not walk on the ground like other birds do. Instead, they spend their time either perching or flying. Once airborne, hummingbirds never glide on the wind; they must continue moving their wings in order to fly.

Hummingbirds, like all birds, are warm-blooded. This means they are able to keep their body temperature at a constant level, no matter what the temperature is outside. Birds may adjust their body temperatures by panting to cool down or shivering to warm up. Some birds, including a number of hummingbird species, even **hibernate** in cold weather. A hummingbird's heart may beat more than 1,000 times per minute, but to conserve energy, a hibernating hummingbird may lower its heart rate to as few as 50 beats per minute.

An active hummingbird expends an enormous amount of energy and must eat two-thirds of its weight in food

The violet-tailed sylph is an abundant hummingbird species found only in the forests of Colombia and Ecuador.

Earth's smallest bird, the bee hummingbird, lives only on Cuba and its neighboring island, Isla de la Juventud.

every day. Hummingbirds are omnivores, meaning they eat both live prey and plant matter. Flowers, **nectar**, and sap provide energy-producing carbohydrates, and insects and spiders provide the fat and protein needed to build up muscles and protect organs. Hummingbirds have some of the strongest chest muscles of all birds. One-third of their body weight is muscle. This is what allows them to be the strongest fliers, despite their small size.

Hummingbirds vary greatly in size. The bee hummingbird of Cuba is the smallest species. Though it weighs just 0.06 ounce (1.7 g)—that's less than the weight of a penny—and its body is just 1 inch (2.5 cm) long, that length is doubled when the bird's tail and beak are included. The largest hummingbird is the giant hummingbird of the Andes, South America's longest mountain chain. Despite growing to more than eight inches (20.3 cm) in length, the giant hummingbird weighs less than three-quarters of an ounce (21.3 g).

The length of a hummingbird's beak depends on the type of flowers on which it typically feeds. Hummingbirds that feed on small, wide blooms have short beaks, but long, tubular blooms require

The sword-billed hummingbird is the only bird species whose beak exceeds the length of its entire body.

hummingbirds to have long and sometimes curved beaks. The amount of curve also depends on the curvature of the flowers, with some beaks being only slightly curved and others sharply curved. For instance, the sword-billed hummingbird's beak is nearly four inches (10.2 cm) long—longer than its body—and curves slightly upward to allow the bird to feed on the hanging blooms of the climbing passionflower, its favorite food.

A hummingbird's beak is made of keratin—the same material found in human fingernails. To feed, the bird opens its beak slightly and extends its long tongue. The

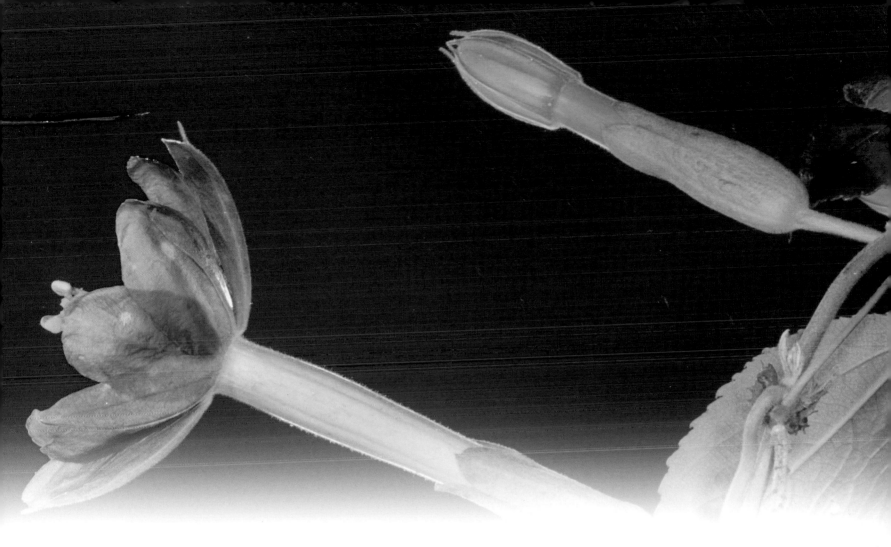

tongue may look like a straw, but a hummingbird does not feed on nectar like a person sucks liquid through a straw. Rather, a hummingbird's tongue forks about halfway down its length. Each fork is slightly grooved and covered with tiny hairs that soak up the nectar—similar to the way a paper towel soaks up spilled liquids. The nectar is then transported along the hairs and into the hummingbird's mouth.

Hummingbirds have no sense of smell, so they hunt for insects and search for flowers using their keen eyesight. Red flowers are always a first choice,

Sword-billed hummingbirds pollinate passionflowers, helping the plants make a fruit that is eaten by wild pigs.

The green hermit's beak is 1.5 inches (4 cm) long and curves downward at a 30-degree angle to better reach nectar.

probably because the color stands out against foliage, but hummingbirds will feed from flowers of any color as long as the sugar content of the nectar is at least 25 percent. A hummingbird has a high **metabolism** and feeds from as many as 1,000 flowers each day.

Unlike other insect-eating birds, hummingbirds cannot capture prey by quickly snapping their mouths shut and catching the bug with the tip of the beak. Their beaks are too long, preventing hummingbirds from moving them with great speed. Instead, a hummingbird's flexible lower beak bends downward and widens, becoming shaped like a catcher's mitt. Insects and spiders are then scooped from the sky or collected from their perches.

Hummingbirds have large eyes set on the sides of the head. This allows them to see both straight ahead and off to the sides. Like those of other birds, hummingbird eyes are protected by a nictitating (*NIK-tih-tayt-ing*) membrane (a see-through inner eyelid). Also, hummingbirds appear to have thick eyelashes, but these are actually tiny tufts of feathers that help protect the eyes from dust and debris while the bird is in flight.

No other birds can fly the way hummingbirds can.

Hummingbirds can zip up, down, sideways, forward, and backward, and they can hover in place. Hummingbirds have shoulder joints that allow them to rotate their wings in a figure-eight pattern. By lifting air with the upstroke and then immediately pushing against the air with the downstroke—at a rate as fast as 80 beats per second—a hummingbird can hover in midair. Hummingbirds fly at an average speed of 30 miles (48 m) per hour, but they can dive at twice that speed.

Migrating between Mexico and southern Alaska, the rufous nests farther north than any other hummingbird.

Male hummingbirds hoping to mate may hover in front of a female to display strength and show off their plumage.

SHIMMERING ACROBATS

Most species of hummingbird have a life span of about four to six years; however, **ornithologists** have discovered some hummingbirds that can live much longer. The Patuxent Wildlife Research Center in Laurel, Maryland, studies bird longevity by banding them with small tags and monitoring them throughout their lives. The center banded a broad-tailed hummingbird in 1976 and then recaptured it 12 years later—making it the longest-lived hummingbird on record.

Hummingbirds reach maturity and are ready to mate at age one. Typically, more females can be found in a given area than males, so a male will mate with several females. To choose a mate, hummingbirds perform courtship rituals known as flight displays. Strong flight skills are indications of a male hummingbird's abilities to produce healthy offspring and defend valuable feeding grounds.

One important flight display is the dive. A male hummingbird flies straight up into the air—as high as 50 feet (15.2 m)—and then dives downward at top speed toward the female. He pulls up at the last moment, right in front of her, beating his wings loudly and vocalizing with

When male hummingbirds pull out of high-speed courtship dives, they experience more than nine times the force of gravity.

chirps and whistles. The male will repeat this maneuver until he believes the female is sufficiently impressed.

As part of the courtship, the male may hover in midair directly in front of the female for several minutes, allowing her to judge his strength and skill. He may then land next to her, turning to poke his beak toward her. If the female does not like the male, she will fly away. But if she is impressed with him, the female will turn to face him, and the two birds will flash their beaks toward one another. They may huddle close together and rest for a time before mating. After mating, the female busies herself with nest building, while the male flies off in search of other females in the area.

Sometimes hummingbirds reuse nests from the previous year or rebuild damaged nests. When a new nest is required, a hummingbird usually selects a forked branch that is located over a water source or an open area. This location gives the bird a clear view of any approaching predator. Some species build round nests that hang suspended from tree limbs or are attached to the sides of buildings, but the glittering emerald hummingbird makes her nest among draping vines so that it hangs like a tiny

baskct. Nests of different shapes are built by other species, such as the hermit hummingbird, whose cone-shaped nest hangs from the underside of vegetation.

A female carrying eggs spends up to seven days building her nest. Working several hours a day, she makes dozens of trips each hour with building materials in her mouth. These can include plant matter, tree bark, **lichens** (*LY-kenz*), feathers, and fur. As she places all of the pieces in just the right spots, the female hummingbird binds everything together with sticky silk she has carefully collected from spider webs.

Touching each other's beaks, or bills, is called billing, and it strengthens the bond between mating pairs.

The rare and endangered marvelous spatuletail is found only in a remote river valley in northern Peru.

A typical round hummingbird nest measures about 2.5 inches (6.4 cm) high; it is only about 1.5 inches (3.8 cm) wide inside. Some are slightly larger, and some are slightly smaller. The hummingbird molds the soft nest into the perfect shape by pressing her body against its inner walls and pulling at its edges with her wings and tail feathers. She uses her feet to press down the floor. Then she lays her eggs—2 of them laid 48 hours apart.

The nest is large enough to accommodate only the two pea-sized eggs and the mother hummingbird. The mother will not leave her nest for more than 10 minutes each hour— just enough time to find food in order to keep her energy level high. Her mate defends the feeding grounds from rival males, so the female does not need to search far for food.

Like all birds' eggs, hummingbird eggs must be incubated, or kept warm, while the baby hummingbirds are developing inside. Depending on the species, hummingbirds must incubate their eggs for two to three weeks. At birth, the baby hummingbird chips through the hard shell of its egg using its **egg tooth**. It has no **down** and emerges featherless and blind. Most species weigh less than two-tenths of an ounce (5.7 g). They rely entirely on the mother for warmth and protection. The mother can leave her babies for only minutes at a time to forage for food.

Hummingbirds grow quickly, doubling in size within three days. In another three days they double again, and by day eight, their first feathers emerge. By this time, the hatchlings can stay warm in the nest, while their mother flies off for longer periods of time to collect food for them.

A mother hummingbird must partially digest the food she collects in order to feed her young. She gathers small insects, nectar, and pollen in her **crop** and carries it to her nest, where she regurgitates the softened mixture into the mouths of her offspring. They are voracious eaters and are

Hummingbird nests are usually too fragile to survive for more than one breeding season.

The marvelous spatuletail hummingbird of Peru has two long tail feathers ending in large discs that can be moved independently.

A hummingbird nest containing two chicks is light and may weigh only about one quarter of an ounce (7 g).

almost constantly hungry because they require a great deal of energy to grow as quickly as they do. At two weeks of age, the young hummingbirds have a complete set of new feathers, and they practice beating their wings to exercise their muscles. They continue to grow and strengthen their bodies for another one to two weeks. Then, at nearly a month of age, the young hummingbirds are ready to leave the nest and begin foraging on their own.

The **mortality rate** of hummingbird hatchlings is high. Only about half survive their first year. Squirrels and other small **mammals**, snakes, or even insects may raid nests for the eggs. Young hummingbirds may simply make mistakes when foraging for food and fail to gather sufficient **nutrients** to survive. Because they are so quick, flying hummingbirds are relatively safe. A sleeping hummingbird, though, may be preyed upon by snakes and larger birds—particularly kestrels, which are small, swift birds of prey. Some of the smallest hummingbird species even fall victim to mantises—predatory insects that may sit like statues on flowers or leaves, waiting for a hummingbird to come close enough to be grabbed. Hummingbirds can also succumb to illness, such as avian pox, or various fungal infections.

Colombia's gorgeted puffleg hummingbird was discovered in 2005, yet it is already endangered due to deforestation.

The Nazca hummingbird is as long as New York's Empire State Building is tall—1,250 feet (381 m).

HUMMINGBIRD WARRIORS

Male hummingbirds will fight over females, and both sexes will battle furiously over territory and food.

The hummingbird is a symbol of strength and speed in many **cultures** of the world. Though it is small and generally peaceful, the hummingbird will defend its territory and nest to the death. For this reason, the Taino people of the Caribbean—the first to be encountered by Christopher Columbus on his first voyage to the New World in 1492—called their fighters the Hummingbird Warriors, peaceful young men who would, when needed, defend their homeland from invaders with courage and strength of spirit. The Taino also believed that hummingbirds were symbols of rebirth, spreading life across the land.

When the tribe of Aztec people called the Mexica dominated southern Mexico from the 1300s through the early 1500s, the national god Huitzilopochtli, whose name means "Left-handed Hummingbird," guided their culture. The Mexica believed that Huitzilopochtli, who was also god of the sun and war, would lead the souls of men who died in war across the sky and transform them into hummingbirds.

Perhaps one of the oldest and most mysterious examples of hummingbirds' influence on human culture is the

Images of Huitzilopochtli depict this Aztec god wearing a cloak and headpiece adorned with bird feathers.

enormous hummingbird drawn into the desert of southern Peru. Part of the Nazca Lines, a series of geoglyphs, or drawings etched into the ground, the outline of the hummingbird was created by scraping off the red desert earth to reveal the white rock underneath. The etchings are more than 2,000 years old and were crafted by the Nazca people between 200 B.C. and A.D. 600.

Because the designs of the Nazca Lines—which also include the figures of a monkey, a spider, and a tree, among other objects—are not evident from the ground, they were not discovered until the 1920s, when airplanes first flew over the desert. No one knows for sure why the Nazca people made such enormous artwork that they could not even fully see, but most researchers agree that the geoglyphs had some sort of spiritual significance, as Nazca graves have been found near the geoglyphs.

The hummingbird is a sacred symbol to many **indigenous** peoples of North and South America. Because the hummingbird is considered to be a joyful worker, the Haida people of the Pacific Northwest region of North America think of it as a symbol of good luck and joy. A story from the **mythology** of the Hopi and Zuni

Hummingbirds are commonly depicted on ancient artifacts such as this jug made by the Nazca people.

American Indian tribes explains how the hummingbird brought rain from the gods to help humans. To this day, potters often decorate water jugs with images of hummingbirds to show gratitude for the bird's gift.

Some cultures loved hummingbirds excessively. The Purépecha people ruled a vast area of southern Mexico's Pacific coast before the days of the Spanish explorers in the 1500s. A century before, the city of Tzintzuntzan, or "Place of the Hummingbirds," was a thriving capital that featured large stone temples and platforms. The people prized hummingbirds for their spectacular coloring and created clothing and ornaments adorned with thousands of shimmering hummingbird feathers. Unfortunately, this led to the **extinction** of hummingbirds in the area, and the city fell into ruin in the early 16th century.

Some cultures also believed that hummingbirds had magical properties and used their bones and organs in traditional medicines. It was also widely believed that hummingbirds brought good luck, and people would wear stuffed hummingbirds around their necks as lucky charms. An example of this can be seen in Mexican artist Frida Kahlo's 1940 painting *Self-Portrait with Thorn*

Necklace and Hummingbird, which is owned by the Harry Ransom Center at the University of Texas at Austin.

Today, admirers of hummingbirds draw them to yards and gardens with hummingbird feeders. Bostonian Laurence J. Webster designed the first modern hummingbird feeder in the early 1930s after seeing an article in *National Geographic* about hummingbirds being fed from glass bottles. The public got a good look at Webster's feeder in 1947, when *National Geographic* published a story about a new invention used in photography, the strobe flash. The technology was demonstrated by capturing images of hummingbirds at one of Webster's feeders. Since then, hummingbird feeders have become enormously popular and can be found in a wide range of designs, from plastic trays that hold inverted soda bottles to exquisite blown-glass works of art.

One thing that hummingbird fanciers have learned from the experience of luring the tiny birds within view relates to color. Because hummingbirds are more attracted to red than any other color, many hummingbird feeders feature that color. Although a hummingbird can feed while hovering in the air, the best hummingbird feeders

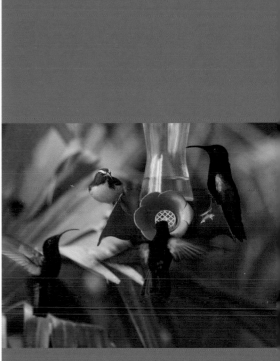

Flicking their tongues with incredible speed, hummingbirds consume nectar at the rate of about 13 licks per second.

By providing constant care, people have often rescued and rehabilitated orphaned and injured hummingbirds.

are designed with perches, which can help the birds conserve an enormous amount of energy while feeding. People can buy hummingbird food, but most simply create a mixture of one part white sugar to four parts clean water to make hummingbird food that is similar to flower nectar.

Several recent books have captured the spirit of the hummingbird. *The Magic Hummingbird: A Hopi Folktale* (1995) by Ekkehart Malotki and Michael Lomatuway'Ma is an American Indian pourquoi, or origin, story that tells how the hummingbird brought food and water to the people. A 1995 story collection by Linda Yamane includes the tale of how the hummingbird brought fire to the Ohlone, the indigenous people of northern California. And Michael Rose Ramirez's *The Legend of the Hummingbird: A Tale from Puerto Rico* (1998) recounts a traditional folk tale about a boy and girl from rival tribes who fall in love. To remain together, the girl becomes a red flower, and the boy becomes a hummingbird.

Hummingbirds do not often appear in films, but one was featured in the 1995 animated Disney movie *Pocahontas*. Flit, a hummingbird with a strong sense

of independence, is a friend of the main character, an American Indian girl named Pocahontas, and he often lands on her hand to give her advice. In real life, most wild birds will avoid humans at all costs, but hummingbirds can learn to trust people, perching on the hands of those who provide them with food. They can even be **conditioned** to remember places and individuals, returning year after year to provide living color to our world.

A group of hummingbirds is sometimes referred to as a hover, a bouquet, a shimmer, or even a tune.

HUMMING-BIRD

I can imagine, in some otherworld
Primeval-dumb, far back
In that most awful stillness, that only gasped and hummed,
Humming-birds raced down the avenues.

Before anything had a soul,
While life was a heave of Matter, half inanimate,
This little bit chipped off in brilliance
And went whizzing through the slow, vast, succulent stems.

I believe there were no flowers, then,
In the world where the humming-bird flashed ahead of creation.
I believe he pierced the slow vegetable veins with his long beak.

Probably he was big
As mosses, and little lizards, they say were once big.
Probably he was a jabbing, terrifying monster.
We look at him through the wrong end of the long telescope of Time,
Luckily for us.

by D. H. Lawrence (1885–1930)

HIGHFLYING HUMMERS

Scientists believe all birds **evolved** from hollow-boned reptiles that existed millions of years ago. The link between these two kinds of animals is the *Archaeopteryx*, a creature with feathered wings and reptilian teeth. It died out about 146 million years ago, but other birdlike creatures continued to evolve. While hummingbirds today exist only in the Americas, fossils indicate that early hummingbird ancestors lived in Europe about 30 million years ago. Scientists believe that a primitive bird called *Eurotrochilus* is a direct hummingbird ancestor because, among other characteristics, this bird had a long, narrow beak; a wide, U-shaped furcula (commonly known as a wishbone); and very thin legs—just like modern hummingbirds.

Research indicates that, as the last continental glaciers began moving across Europe about 2.5 million years ago, the flowering plants on which early hummingbirds fed died out. The birds were forced to find food sources elsewhere, traveling southward around the globe. The hummingbirds that settled in South America were the only ones to survive Earth's changing climate, and as they

Several varieties of coquette hummingbirds have colored head crests that stand up when the birds are alarmed or excited.

The green-throated carib can be found at low elevations in Puerto Rico and the Lesser Antilles.

continued to evolve, they moved into North America as well. As **pollinators**, these early hummingbirds were responsible for influencing the evolution of the plants on which they fed. Over millions of years, the number of hummingbird species increased, and they became specialized feeders.

An example of specialized feeding can be observed in the habits of the purple-throated carib hummingbird, which is native to mountain forests and clearings throughout the Caribbean islands known as the Lesser Antilles. The male of this species, which has a straight beak, feeds on the yellow flowers of the *Heliconia caribaea*, whose long, straight flower petals look like lobster claws. The female purple-throated carib has a long, curved beak that matches the flower structure of the red *Heliconia bihai*. The Heliconia species, which rely on hummingbirds as their sole pollinators, have evolved to match the needs of hummingbirds on various Caribbean islands, a process called coadaptation. On the island of St. Lucia, for example, in areas where *Heliconia caribaea* is rare, the *Heliconia bihai* has adapted by evolving a yellow-colored variety that attracts males, who would otherwise have fewer food sources, while still maintaining the shape favored by females.

While warm-weather hummingbirds such as the purple-throated carib remain in their habitats year round, most North American species migrate seasonally, following the same routes year after year. Research on hummingbird migration can be a collaborative effort between nations. The Holiday Beach Migration Observatory, located in southwestern Ontario, works with an organization headquartered just across Lake Erie in Michigan called Great Lakes HummerNet and with Operation Ruby Throat, headquartered in York, South Carolina, to track the migration patterns of ruby-throated hummingbirds as they travel back and forth between Canada and the southern United States.

Such research involves a process called banding. Birds are caught by various methods, including trapping and netting. Then the birds' legs are fitted with a metal or plastic bracelet, called a band, which is imprinted with a number or code. The bird is released, and then over a period of months or years, the bird is recaptured and identified by its band. This method of gathering data

Global warming can affect hummingbird migration by causing some species to stray from their normal range, where food may be in short supply.

Hummingbirds can see colors on the ultraviolet end of the **spectrum**, but humans can see only the violet end.

works well to keep track of birds that continually travel from place to place.

Because hummingbirds are so small and fragile, capturing them requires great care. The most common method of capture involves the use of mist nets, which resemble volleyball nets in structure. Nearly invisible nylon netting is strung between two poles and surrounds hummingbird feeders on three sides and the top. This allows the birds access to—and escape from—the feeders from only one direction, making it easy for researchers to drive the birds into the netting. Even if a hummingbird detects the netting on one side, it often cannot avoid being caught on one of the other sides or at the top. Researchers immediately remove the trapped hummingbird so it does not become entangled, which can damage its fragile wings.

After a hummingbird is captured, the first step is to place it in a soft pouch to keep it calm while researchers handle it. If a bird has not already been banded, it will be fitted with a tiny band, and if a bird's age and sex can be determined, this information will be recorded. Sex may be indicated by the bird's body length and beak length,

which are precisely measured. The tail length is also measured. Lastly, the hummingbird is weighed. A ruby-throated hummingbird typically weighs no more than a nickel. It can weigh from less than one-tenth of an ounce to one-eighth of an ounce (2.8–3.5 g) in the summer, and it gains up to an additional one-twentieth of an ounce (1.4 g) during migration.

After all of the data on a captured hummingbird is gathered and recorded, the researchers give the bird a drink of sugar water for an energy boost, then release it. The entire process takes only a few minutes, and the

Scientists estimate that a ruby-throated hummingbird can fly across the Gulf of Mexico in about 20 hours.

The Costas hummingbird lives in arid regions of the American West, feeding on the nectar of flowering cholla cacti.

bird is unharmed. After a period of months, the process begins again, with the birds being recaptured to record additional data such as growth, feather damage, and beak wear. To save time—and to avoid undue stress on hummingbirds—bands may be painted with a particular color each time the bird is captured to help researchers know if a bird has been recently recaptured and its information recorded. If a recently recaptured bird is caught, it can be immediately released.

One of the most successful ongoing hummingbird studies has been taking place at the Arizona–Sonora Desert Museum in Tucson, where the Hummingbird Aviary is home to Costas, broad-billed, black-chinned, Anna's, and calliope hummingbirds that fly free inside a huge, climate-controlled enclosure. Researchers there have observed hummingbird mating, nest building, and raising of offspring. More than 100 baby hummingbirds have hatched in the aviary since it opened in 1988.

Wherever hummingbirds are found, they must compete with humans for habitat. In places all around the world, trees that hummingbirds need for nesting are cut down, and dams are built, flooding the meadows and prairies where hummingbirds feed. While most hummingbird species exist in healthy numbers, many have been forced to leave their native lands and are considered vulnerable. Continued research and education on the needs and habits of hummingbirds is essential in keeping these jewels of the sky flying high.

Hummingbirds have a colored throat patch called a gorget, named for the steel or leather collar in military armor that protects the throat.

ANIMAL TALE: HOW THE HUMMINGBIRD GOT HER COLORS

The hummingbird is unique in terms of its flying abilities, but it is also known for its wide range of stunning colors. This tale from the ancient Maya people of Central America tells how the hummingbird came to be one of the best dressed of all birds.

The Great Spirit created Tzunu'un, or hummingbird, as a small, fragile bird who could fly backwards and hover in place—feats that no other birds could perform. But Tzunu'un was a plain-looking bird, drab and gray with dull feathers and awkward feet. Despite this, Tzunu'un was also cheerful and kind, and she took great pride in her flying skills.

Finally the day came when Tzunu'un would take a husband. All of her feathered friends helped her prepare the wedding table and sang joyful songs of love and happy times. But Tzunu'un had nothing special

to wear for her wedding, and despite her normally happy attitude, she felt a little fearful that she would disappoint her new husband, whom the Great Spirit had so generously selected for her.

Tzunu'un's feathered friends decided to make her some wedding clothes. The resplendent quetzal, called Kukul, plucked out some of the brilliant red feathers he wore around his neck and gave them to Tzunu'un for a necklace. She was thrilled.

Then the Yucatan parrot, called T'uut, plucked out some of her brightest green feathers to help make Tzunu'un a gown. The Yucatan jay, called Ch'el, also shared some of the shimmering turquoise feathers from her back and wings to help make the gown.

Not to be outdone, the blue-crowned motmot, Toh, volunteered some of his emerald green and turquoise plumage, as did Ch'ujum, the Yucatan woodpecker,

whose head was covered with brilliant red feathers and whose breast shined with white ones.

Then Yuyum the orange oriole, who was a swift and skilled seamstress, sewed up all of the glorious plumage into a beautiful wedding gown. The spider, called Am, wove a delicate veil.

Soon word of the wedding spread all throughout the forest, and Canac the honeybee gathered all of his friends to bring sweets to the wedding table. They brought honey and nectar in tall vases and strings of Tzunu'un's favorite blooming flowers—bright Mexican sunflowers, red hibiscus, purple orchids, and pink fuchsias.

Finally, all of the sweetest fruit trees, including the orange, guava, papaya, and banana, filled the wedding table with ripe fruits for the guests to enjoy, while Ukum the band-tailed pigeon sang wedding songs, and all of the butterflies of the forest gathered to dance for Tzunu'un and her husband.

The wedding was a great success, with the sweetest flowers and food, loveliest music, and most adoring friends that Tzunu'un could have ever wished to have. She was so touched and so happy that she flapped her wings furiously, zigzagging from friend to friend with great speed to thank them all, over and over again.

The Great Spirit was so pleased by the gratitude with which Tzunu'un showered her friends that he sent his messenger, Cozumel the swallow, to tell Tzunu'un that she would be allowed to wear her colorful wedding garments for the rest of her life. And to this day, she does wear them—brilliant turquoise, emerald green, white, red, and nearly every other shimmering color of the rainbow.

GLOSSARY

conditioned – made to respond or behave in a certain way as a result of training

crop – a muscular pouch near the throat of some animals and birds used for food storage prior to digestion

cultures – particular groups in a society that share behaviors and characteristics that are accepted as normal by those groups

deforestation – the clearing away of trees from a forest

down – small feathers whose barbs do not interlock to form a flat surface, thus giving a fluffy appearance

egg tooth – a hard, toothlike tip of a young bird's beak or a young reptile's mouth, used only for breaking through its egg

evolved – gradually developed into a new form

extinction – the act or process of becoming extinct; coming to an end or dying out

global warming – the gradual increase in Earth's temperature that causes changes in climates, or long-term weather conditions, around the world

hibernate – to spend the winter in a sleep-like state in which breathing and heart rate slow down

indigenous – originating in a particular region or country

lichens – organisms made up of fungus and algae growing in partnership

mammals – warm-blooded animals that have backbones and hair or fur, give birth to live young, and produce milk to feed their young

metabolism – the processes that keep a body alive, including making use of food for energy

mortality rate – the number of deaths in a certain area or period

mythology – a collection of myths, or popular, traditional beliefs or stories that explain how something came to be or that are associated with a person or object

nectar – the sugary fluid produced by a plant

nutrients – substances that give an animal energy and help it grow

ornithologists – scientists who study birds and their lives

plumage – the entire feathery covering of a bird

pollen – a yellow powder made by flowers that is used to fertilize other flowers

pollinators – animals or insects that transfer pollen from plant to plant, aiding in plant reproduction

spectrum – a range of qualities in related items such as light waves or sound waves

SELECTED BIBLIOGRAPHY

Chambers, Lanny. "About Hummingbirds." Hummingbirds.net. http://hummingbirds.net/about.html.

Gates, Larry, and Terrie Gates. "The Hummingbird Web Site." Hummingbird World. http://hummingbirdworld.com/h/.

Howell, Steve. *Hummingbirds of North America: A Photographic Guide*. Princeton: Princeton University Press, 2003.

Kaminski, Thomas. *Hummingbirds! Beauty and the Beast*. VHS. Rolling Hills Estates, Calif.: Avian Video Center, 2009.

Tilford, Tony. *The Complete Book of Hummingbirds*. San Diego: Thunder Bay Press, 2009.

Toops, Connie. *Hummingbirds: Jewels in Flight*. Osceola, Wisc.: Voyageur Press, 2005.

The Butterfly and Hummingbird Garden in Michigan's Detroit Zoo is home to a handful of birds from Peru.

INDEX